easy meals

Vegetarian

p

This is a Parragon Publishing Book
First printed in 2001

Parragon Publishing
Queen Street House
4 Queen Street
Bath BA1 1HE
United Kingdom

ISBN: 0-75255-774-2

Printed in Spain

Produced by The Bridgewater Book Company Ltd, Lewes, East Sussex, United Kingdom

Creative Director Terry Jeavons
Art Director Sarah Howerd
Editorial Director Fiona Biggs
Senior Editor Mark Truman
Editorial Assistant Tom Kitch
Page Make-up Sara Kidd

NOTES FOR THE READER

- This book uses both metric and US measurements. Follow the same units of
  measurement throughout; do not mix metric and US.
- All spoon measurements are level: teaspoons are assumed to be 5 ml, and
  tablespoons are assumed to be 15 ml.
- Cup measurements in this book are for American cups.
- Unless otherwise stated, milk is assumed to be whole milk, eggs and individual
  vegetables such as potatoes are medium-sized, and pepper is freshly ground
  black pepper.
- Recipes using raw or very lightly cooked eggs should be avoided by infants, the
  elderly, pregnant women, convalescents, and anyone suffering from an illness.
- Optional ingredients, variations, and serving suggestions have not been included
  in the calculations. The times given are an approximate guide only. Preparation
  times differ according to the techniques used by different people and the cooking
  times vary as a result of the type of oven used.

Contents

Introduction

A vegetarian diet needs planning to ensure that it includes all the essential nutrients. If you are a vegetarian and often find yourself short of time to plan a meal, you may habitually fall back on fast foods which do not make up a balanced diet. The cheese and tomato sandwich you have for lunch may look completely different from the cheese and tomato pizza you have for dinner, but they have essentially the same nutritional value.

The recipes in the following pages have been chosen to ensure that your meals are not only nutritious and simple to prepare for a quick lunch or supper, but that they are also inspiring. The recipes include plenty of protein in the form of a wide range of beans, nuts, and grains such as rice, barley, and wheat, and vitamins, minerals and calcium from many different sources, plus rich and exotic flavorings from herbs and spices. This wide

guide to recipe key	
easy	Recipes are graded as follows: 1 pea—easy; 2 peas—very easy; 3 peas—extremely easy.
serves 4	Most of the recipes in this book serve four people. Simply halve the ingredients to serve two, taking care not to mix US and metric measurements.
15 minutes	Preparation time. Where recipes include marinating, soaking, standing, or chilling, times for these are listed separately: eg, 15 minutes, plus 30 minutes to marinate.
15 minutes	Cooking time. Cooking times do not include the cooking of rice or noodles served with the main dishes.

variety of ingredients is the basis for a rich store of new ideas for dishes which are all easy to cook.

The recipes come from all over the world, so there is plenty of scope for creating interesting menus. A smooth vegetable soup followed by Spicy Cashew Nut Curry, or Vegetable Tostadas served with a salad of mixed greens is one example, sure to be tempting. And guests will be impressed by a classic Greek salad followed by colorful Red Rice Pilaf with Roasted Vegetables, with Almond Rice Custard or Chocolate Hazelnut Pots to finish.

Omelet Stuffed with Eggplants and Mushrooms, page 44

Soups & Appetizers

The soups in this section range from classics, such as Spinach, to a spicy Mexican Vegetable Soup with tortilla chips. Barley & Rice Soup with Chard is substantial enough to make a light lunch dish. Similarly, hummus—an appetizer made from garbanzo beans and tahini (crushed sesame seeds), flavored with garlic, olive oil and lemon—may be served as a dip, but it is full of protein and calcium, and served with pitas and crisp raw vegetables, it makes a one-dish meal.

Spinach Soup

1 tbsp olive oil
1 onion, halved and
  sliced thinly
1 leek, split lengthwise
  and sliced thinly
1 potato, diced finely
4 cups water
2 sprigs fresh marjoram
  or ¼ tsp dried
2 sprigs fresh thyme or
  ¼ tsp dried
1 bay leaf
14 oz/400 g young
  spinach, washed
freshly grated nutmeg
salt and pepper
4 tbsp light cream, to
  serve

❶ Heat the oil in a heavy-based pan over a medium heat. Add the onion and leek and cook for about 3 minutes, stirring occasionally, until they begin to soften.

❷ Add the potato, water, marjoram, thyme, and bay leaf, and a pinch of salt. Bring to a boil, reduce the heat, then cover and cook gently for about 25 minutes, or until the vegetables are tender. Remove the bay leaf and herb stems.

❸ Add the spinach and continue cooking for 3–4 minutes, stirring frequently, just until it is completely wilted.

❹ Let the soup cool slightly, then transfer to a blender or a food processor and blend until smooth, working in batches if necessary. (If using a food processor, strain off the cooking liquid and reserve. Purée the soup solids with enough cooking liquid to moisten them, then combine with the remaining liquid.)

❺ Return the soup to the pan and if it is too thick, thin it with a little more water. Season with salt, a good grinding of pepper, and a generous grating of nutmeg. Place over a low heat and simmer until reheated.

❻ Ladle the soup into warm bowls and swirl a tablespoonful of cream into each serving.

very easy

serves 4

15 minutes

45 minutes

Roasted Pumpkin & Tomato Soup

INGREDIENTS

1–2 tbsp olive oil
2 lb/900 g peeled
  pumpkin flesh, cut
  into slices ¾ inch/2 cm
  thick
1 lb/450 g ripe tomatoes,
  skinned, cored, and
  sliced thickly
1 onion, chopped
2 garlic cloves, chopped
  finely
4 tbsp white wine
2 tbsp water
2½ cups vegetable
  bouillon
½ cup light cream
salt and pepper
snipped chives, to
  garnish

❶ Drizzle 1 tablespoon of the olive oil over the base of a large baking dish. Place the pumpkin, tomatoes, onion, and garlic in it, forming 2 or 3 layers. Drizzle the top with the remaining olive oil, then pour the wine and water over the top. Season with a little salt and pepper.

❷ Cover the dish with kitchen foil and bake in a preheated oven at 375°F/190°C for about 45 minutes, or until all the vegetables are soft.

❸ Let the vegetables cool slightly, then transfer to a blender or a food processor and add the cooking juices and as much bouillon as needed to cover the vegetables. Purée until smooth, working in batches if necessary.

❹ Pour the purée into a pan and stir in the remaining bouillon. Cook gently over a medium heat, stirring occasionally, for about 15 minutes, or until heated through. Stir in the cream and continue cooking for 3–4 minutes.

❺ Taste and adjust the seasoning, if necessary. Ladle the soup into warm bowls, garnish with chives, and serve.

very easy

serves 4

25 minutes

1 hour 5 minutes

Beans & Greens Soup

INGREDIENTS

*9 oz/250 g dried Great
  Northern or cannellini
  beans*
1 tbsp olive oil
2 onions, chopped finely
*4 garlic cloves, chopped
  finely*
*1 celery stalk, sliced
  thinly*
*2 carrots, halved and
  sliced thinly*
5 cups water
¼ tsp dried thyme
¼ tsp dried marjoram
1 bay leaf
*4½ oz/125 g leafy greens,
  such as Swiss chard,
  mustard, spinach, and
  kale, washed*
salt and pepper

❶ Pick over the beans, then cover with cold water and let soak for 6 hours or overnight. Drain the beans and put in a pan, then add enough cold water to cover by 2 inches/5 cm. Bring to a boil, and boil for 10 minutes. Drain and rinse.

❷ Heat the oil in a pan, then add the onion and cook, covered, for 3–4 minutes, stirring occasionally, until just softened. Add the garlic, celery, and carrots, and cook for 2 minutes.

❸ Add the water, beans, thyme, marjoram, and bay leaf. When the mixture bubbles, reduce the heat. Cover and simmer, stirring occasionally, for 1¼ hours, or until the beans are tender (the cooking time varies with the type of bean). Season to taste.

❹ Let the soup cool slightly, then transfer 2 cups to a blender or a food processor. Blend until smooth and recombine with the soup.

❺ Cut the greens crosswise into thin ribbons, a handful at a time. Keep spinach and other tender leaves separate. Add the thicker leaves to the soup and cook gently, uncovered, for 10 minutes. Stir in any remaining greens and continue cooking for 5–10 minutes, or until all the greens are tender.

❻ Taste and adjust the seasoning, if necessary. Ladle the soup into warm bowls and serve.

easy

serves 4

15 minutes

2 hours

Barley & Rice Soup with Swiss Chard

INGREDIENTS

3½ oz/100 g pearl barley
3½ oz/100 g long-grain brown rice
1 lb/450 g Swiss chard, trimmed and soaked for 10 minutes
2 tbsp olive oil
1 large onion, chopped finely
2 carrots, chopped finely
2 celery stalks, chopped finely
2 garlic cloves, chopped finely
14 oz/400 g canned chopped Italian plum tomatoes with their juice
1 bay leaf
1 tsp dried thyme
1 tsp herbes de Provence or dried oregano
4 cups vegetable bouillon
1 lb/450 g canned cannellini beans, drained
2 tbsp chopped fresh parsley
salt and pepper
freshly grated Parmesan cheese, to serve

very easy

serves 4

15 minutes

1½ hours

❶ Bring a large pan of water to a boil. Add the barley and the brown rice, and return to a boil. Reduce the heat and simmer gently for 30–35 minutes, or until just tender. Drain and set aside.

❷ Drain the Swiss chard. Cut out the hard white stems and slice the stems crosswise into very thin strips, then set the strips aside. Roll the leaves into a long cigar shape and shred them thinly, then set the rolled leaves aside.

❸ Heat the oil in a large pan. Add the onion, carrots, and celery, and cook, stirring frequently, for about 5 minutes, or until soft and beginning to color. Add the garlic and cook for a minute longer. Add the tomatoes and their juice, the bay leaf, thyme, and herbes de Provence. Reduce the heat and simmer, partially covered, for about 7 minutes, or until all the vegetables are soft.

❹ Stir in the sliced white Swiss chard stems and the bouillon. Simmer gently for about 20 minutes. Add the shredded green Swiss chard and simmer for another 15 minutes.

❺ Stir in the beans and parsley with the cooked barley and brown rice. Season with salt and pepper. Bring back to a boil and simmer for another 8–10 minutes. Serve immediately, with Parmesan cheese for sprinkling.

Mexican Vegetable Soup with Tortilla Chips

INGREDIENTS

2 tbsp vegetable or
   extra-virgin olive oil
1 onion, chopped finely
4 garlic cloves, chopped
   finely
¼–½ tsp ground cumin
2–3 tsp mild chili
   powder, such as ancho
   or New Mexico
1 carrot, sliced
1 waxy potato, diced
1½ cups diced fresh or
   canned tomatoes
1 zucchini, diced
¼ small cabbage, shredded
4 cups vegetable
   bouillon or water
1 corn cob, the kernels
   cut off the cob, or 8
   oz/225 g canned corn
about 10 green or runner
   beans, trimmed, then cut
   into bite-sized lengths
salt and pepper

TO SERVE
4–6 tbsp chopped fresh
   cilantro
salsa of your choice, or
   chopped fresh chili, to
   taste
tortilla chips

❶ Heat the oil in a heavy-based pan. Add the onion and garlic and cook for a few minutes until softened, then sprinkle in the cumin and chili powder. Stir in the carrot, potato, tomatoes, zucchini, and cabbage, and cook for 2 minutes, stirring the mixture occasionally.

❷ Pour in the bouillon. Cover, and cook over a medium heat for 20 minutes, or until the vegetables are tender.

❸ Add extra water if necessary, then stir in the corn and green beans and cook for another 5–10 minutes, or until the beans are tender. Season with salt and pepper to taste, bearing in mind that the tortilla chips may be salty.

❹ Ladle the soup into soup bowls and sprinkle each portion with fresh cilantro. Top with a dab of salsa, then add a handful of tortilla chips.

very easy

serves 4

25 minutes

35 minutes

Hummus

INGREDIENTS

7 oz/200 g dried
  garbanzo beans
2 large garlic cloves
7 tbsp extra-virgin olive
  oil
2½ tbsp tahini
1 tbsp lemon juice, or
  to taste
salt and pepper

TO GARNISH
extra-virgin olive oil
paprika
fresh cilantro

❶ Place the garbanzo beans in a large bowl. Pour in at least twice the volume of cold water to beans and let stand for at least 12 hours, or until they double in size.

❷ Drain the garbanzo beans. Put them in a large flameproof casserole or a pan and add twice the volume of water to beans. Bring to a boil and boil hard for 10 minutes, skimming any scum that forms on the surface.

❸ Lower the heat and let simmer for 1 hour, skimming the surface if necessary, or until the garbanzo beans are tender. Meanwhile, cut the garlic cloves in half and remove the pale green or white cores, then chop coarsely. Set aside.

❹ Drain the garbanzo beans, reserving 4 tablespoons of the cooking liquid. Put the olive oil, garlic, tahini, and lemon juice in a food processor and blend to a smooth paste.

❺ Add the garbanzo beans and pulse until they are finely ground but the hummus is still lightly textured. Add a little of the reserved cooking liquid if the mixture is too thick. Season with salt and pepper to taste.

❻ Transfer to a bowl, then cover with plastic wrap and chill until ready to serve. To serve, drizzle with olive oil and sprinkle with a little paprika, then garnish with fresh cilantro.

very easy

makes about
1 lb 9 oz/700 g

10 minutes

1½ hours, plus
12 hours to soak

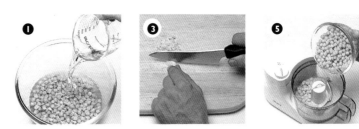

Eggplant Spread

INGREDIENTS

2 large eggplants
1 tomato
1 garlic clove, chopped
4 tbsp extra-virgin olive
   oil
2 tbsp lemon juice
2 tbsp pine nuts, lightly
   toasted
2 scallions, chopped
   finely
salt and pepper

TO GARNISH
ground cumin
2 tbsp chopped finely
   fresh flatleaf parsley

❶ Using a fork or a metal skewer, pierce the eggplants all over. Place them on a cookie sheet in a preheated oven at 450°F/230°C, and roast for 20–25 minutes, or until they are very soft.

❷ Use a folded dish towel to remove the eggplants from the cookie sheet, and set aside to cool.

❸ Place the tomato in a heatproof bowl, then pour boiling water over to cover it, and let it stand for 30 seconds. Drain it, then plunge the tomato into cold water to prevent it from cooking. Skin the tomato, then cut in half and scoop out the seeds with a teaspoon. Dice the flesh finely and set it aside for later use.

❹ Cut the eggplants in half lengthwise. Scoop out the flesh with a spoon and transfer to a food processor. Add the garlic, olive oil, lemon juice, pine kernels, and salt and pepper to taste. Process until smooth.

❺ Spoon the mixture into a bowl and stir in the scallions and diced tomato. Cover, and chill the spread for 30 minutes before serving.

❻ Garnish the dip with a pinch of ground cumin and the chopped parsley, then serve.

very easy

makes about
14 oz/400 g

15 minutes

20–25 minutes

Greek Salad

INGREDIENTS

9 oz/250 g feta cheese
9 oz/250 g cucumber
9 oz/250 g Greek
    kalamata olives
1 red onion or 4 scallions
2 large juicy tomatoes
1 tsp honey
4 tbsp extra-virgin olive
    oil
½ lemon
salt and pepper
fresh or dried oregano,
    to garnish
pitas, to serve

❶ Drain the feta cheese if it is packed in brine. Place it on a cutting board and cut into ½ inch/1 cm dice. Transfer to a salad bowl.

❷ Cut the cucumber in half lengthwise and use a teaspoon to scoop out the seeds. Cut the flesh into ½ inch/1 cm slices. Add to the bowl with the feta cheese.

❸ Pit the olives with an olive or cherry pitter and add them to the salad bowl. Slice the red onion or chop the white and green parts of the scallions finely, and add to the bowl.

❹ Cut each tomato into quarters and scoop out the seeds with a teaspoon. Cut the flesh into bite-sized pieces and add to the bowl.

❺ Using your hands, toss all the ingredients gently together. Stir the honey into the olive oil (see Cook's Tip), then add to the salad and squeeze in lemon juice to taste. Season to taste with pepper and a little salt. Cover, and chill until required.

extremely easy

serves 4

30 minutes

0 minutes

❻ When ready to serve, garnish the chilled salad with the oregano and serve it with pitas.

COOK'S TIP
The small amount of honey helps to bring out the full flavor of the tomatoes.

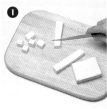

Sweet Potato Cakes with Soy & Tomato Sauce

INGREDIENTS

2 sweet potatoes,
    1 lb 2 oz/500 g total
    weight
2 garlic cloves, crushed
1 small green chile,
    chopped
2 sprigs cilantro,
    chopped
1 tbsp dark soy sauce
all-purpose flour for
    shaping
vegetable oil for frying
sesame seeds for
    sprinkling

SOY & TOMATO SAUCE
2 tsp vegetable oil
1 garlic clove, chopped
    finely
3/4 inch/2 cm piece fresh
    ginger root, chopped
    finely
3 tomatoes, skinned and
    chopped
2 tbsp dark soy sauce
1 tbsp lime juice
2 tbsp fresh cilantro,
    chopped

❶ To make the Soy & Tomato Sauce, heat the oil in a wok and stir-fry the garlic and ginger for about 1 minute. Add the tomatoes and stir-fry for another 2 minutes. Remove from the heat and stir in the soy, lime, and cilantro. Set aside and keep warm.

❷ Peel the sweet potatoes and grate finely (you can do this quickly with a food processor). Place the garlic, chile, and cilantro in a mortar and crush with a pestle to a smooth paste. Stir in the soy sauce mix with the sweet potatoes.

❸ Divide the mixture into 12 equal portions. Dip into flour and pat into a flat, round patty shape.

❹ Heat a shallow pool of oil in a wide skillet. Cook the sweet potato patties over a high heat until they are golden, turning them once.

❺ Drain the cooked patties on paper towels and sprinkle with sesame seeds. Serve while still hot, with a spoonful of the Soy & Tomato Sauce.

easy

serves 4

25 minutes

20 minutes

Main Meals

Cultures that are not predominantly vegetarian often come up with some of the most tempting meat-free dishes. A perfect example of this is Spanakopittas, a delicious crisp pastry stuffed with spinach and feta cheese, sold in generous slices in Greek bakeries throughout the day; while a basic Italian risotto can be dressed up with different vegetables and cheeses to make an elegant but very satisfying vegetarian meal – try Wild Arugula & Tomato Risotto with Mozzarella.

Vegetable Chili

INGREDIENTS

1 medium eggplant,
  peeled if wished, cut
  into 1 inch/2.5 cm
  slices
1 tbsp olive oil, plus extra
  for brushing
1 large red or yellow
  onion, chopped finely
2 bell peppers, chopped
  finely
3–4 garlic cloves,
  chopped finely or
  crushed
28 oz/800 g canned
  chopped tomatoes in
  juice
1 tbsp mild chili powder,
  or to taste
½ tsp ground cumin
½ tsp dried oregano
2 small zucchini,
  quartered lengthwise
  and sliced
14 oz/400 g canned
  kidney beans, drained
  and rinsed
2 cups water
1 tbsp tomato paste
6 scallions, chopped
  finely
4 oz/115 g grated
  Cheddar cheese
salt and pepper

very easy

serves 4

15 minutes

1½ hours

❶ Brush the eggplant slices on one side with olive oil. Heat half the oil in a large skillet over a medium–high heat. Add the eggplant, oiled side up, and cook for 5–6 minutes, or until browned on one side. Turn and brown the other side, then transfer to a plate. Cut into bite-sized pieces.

❷ Heat the remaining oil in a large pan over a medium heat. Add the onion and bell peppers, then cover and cook for 3–4 minutes, stirring occasionally, until the onion is just softened. Add the garlic and continue cooking for 2–3 minutes, or until the onion begins to color.

❸ Add the chopped tomatoes with their juice, and the chili powder, cumin, and oregano to the pan. Season with salt and pepper. Bring just to a boil, reduce the heat, then cover and simmer for 15 minutes.

❹ Add the zucchini, eggplant pieces, and beans. Stir in the water and tomato paste. Cover again and continue simmering for about 45 minutes, or until the vegetables are tender. Taste and adjust the seasoning. If it seems too bland, stir in a little more chili powder to intensify the spiciness of the dish.

❺ Season to taste. Ladle into bowls, and top with scallions and cheese.

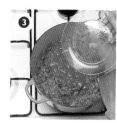

Spanakopittas

INGREDIENTS

2 tbsp olive oil
6 scallions, chopped
9 oz/250 g fresh young
    spinach leaves, tough
    stems removed, rinsed
¼ cup long-grain rice
    (not basmati), boiled
    until tender and
    drained
4 tbsp chopped fresh dill
4 tbsp chopped fresh
    parsley
4 tbsp pine nuts
2 tbsp raisins
2¼ oz/60 g feta cheese,
    drained if necessary
    and crumbled
1 nutmeg
pinch of cayenne pepper
    (optional)
40 sheets phyllo pastry
about 1 cup, plus 2 tbsp
    melted butter
pepper

❶ Heat the oil in a pan, then add the scallions and cook for about 2 minutes. Add the spinach, with the water clinging to the leaves, and cook, stirring, until the leaves wilt. Transfer to a bowl and, when cool enough to handle, squeeze dry.

❷ Stir in the rice, herbs, pine nuts, raisins, and feta cheese. Grate in one-quarter of the nutmeg, and add black and cayenne peppers to taste.

❸ Leave the phyllo sheets in a stack. Cut forty 6 inch/15 cm squares. Remove 8 slices and cut into eight 4 inch/10 cm circles. Re-wrap the unused pastry and cover the squares and circles with a damp dish towel.

❹ Brush a 4 inch/10 cm tart pan with a removable base with butter. Put in one square of phyllo and brush with more butter. Repeat with 7 more sheets. Do not push the phyllo into the ridges.

❺ Spoon in one-fourth of the filling, then top with a phyllo circle and brush with butter. Repeat with another circle. Fold the overhanging phyllo over the top and brush with butter. Make 3 more pies.

❻ Put the pies on a cookie sheet and bake in a preheated oven at 350°F/180°C for 20–25 minutes, or until crisp and golden. Let stand for 5 minutes before turning out.

easy

serves 4

20 minutes

30 minutes

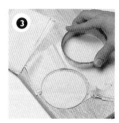

Baked Eggplant Gratin

INGREDIENTS

*1 large eggplant, about
1 lb 12 oz/800 g*
salt
*10½ oz/300 g mozzarella
cheese*
*3 oz/85 g Parmesan
cheese*
olive oil
*1 cup, plus 2 tbsp good-
quality bottled tomato
sauce for pasta*
salt and pepper

❶ Trim the eggplant and cut into ¼ inch/5 mm slices crosswise. Arrange the slices on a large plate, then sprinkle with salt and set aside for 30 minutes to drain.

❷ Meanwhile, drain and grate the mozzarella cheese and grate the Parmesan cheese finely. Set aside.

❸ Rinse the eggplant slices and pat dry with paper towels. Brush a cookie sheet lightly with olive oil and arrange the eggplant slices in one layer. Brush with olive oil.

❹ Roast in a preheated oven at 400°F/200°C for 5 minutes. Using tongs, turn the slices and brush with a little more oil, then bake for another 5 minutes, or until the eggplant is cooked through and tender. Do not switch off the oven.

❺ Spread about 1 tablespoon olive oil over the bottom of a gratin dish or other ovenproof serving dish. Add a layer of eggplant slices, then one-fourth of the tomato sauce and top with one-fourth of the mozzarella. Season to taste with salt and pepper.

❻ Continue layering until all the ingredients are used, ending with a layer of sauce. Sprinkle the Parmesan cheese over the top. Bake in the oven for 30 minutes, or until the cheese bubbles. Let stand for 5 minutes before serving.

very easy

serves 4

20 minutes,
plus 30 minutes
to drain

35 minutes

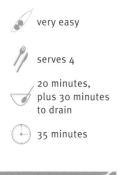

COOK'S TIP
Serve plenty of French
bread with this dish
because it produces the
most delicious juices.

Spiced Lentils with Spinach

INGREDIENTS

2 tbsp olive oil
1 large onion, chopped
    finely
1 large garlic clove,
    crushed
½ tbsp ground cumin
½ tsp ground ginger
9 oz/250 g Puy lentils
about 2½ cups vegetable
    bouillon
3½ oz/100 g baby
    spinach leaves
2 tbsp fresh mint leaves
1 tbsp fresh cilantro
    leaves
1 tbsp fresh flatleaf
    parsley leaves
freshly squeezed lemon
    juice
salt and pepper
grated lemon zest, to
    garnish

❶ Heat the olive oil in a large skillet over a medium–high heat. Add the onion and cook for about 6 minutes. Stir in the garlic, cumin, and ginger, and continue cooking, stirring occasionally, until the onion just starts to brown.

❷ Stir in the lentils. Pour in enough bouillon to cover the lentils by 1 inch/2.5 cm and bring to a boil. Lower the heat and simmer for 20 minutes, or according to the instructions on the packet, until the lentils are tender.

❸ Meanwhile, rinse the spinach leaves in several changes of cold water and shake dry. Chop the mint, cilantro, and parsley leaves finely.

❹ If there is no bouillon left in the pan at this point, add a very small amount, then add the spinach and stir until it just wilts. Stir in the fresh mint, cilantro, and parsley. Adjust the seasoning, adding lemon juice and salt and pepper. Transfer the lentil mixture to a serving bowl and serve, garnished with lemon zest.

very easy

serves 4

10 minutes

45 minutes

❷   ❹   ❹

Hot & Sour Noodles

❶ Cook the noodles in a pan of boiling water for 3–4 minutes, or according to the package directions. Drain well, return to the pan, then toss with the sesame oil and set aside.

❷ Heat the chili oil in a large skillet or wok and quickly stir-fry the garlic, onions, and white mushrooms, to soften but not color them.

❸ Add the black mushrooms, lime juice, soy sauce, and sugar, and continue stir-frying until the mixture is boiling. Add the noodles and toss to mix.

❹ Serve spooned over Belgian endive, sprinkled with cilantro and peanuts.

extremely easy

serves 4

15 minutes

10 minutes

Mixed Vegetables in Groundnut Sauce

INGREDIENTS

2 carrots, peeled
1 small head cauliflower,
    trimmed
2 small heads green bok
    choy
5½ oz/150 g green
    beans, trimmed, if
    preferred
2 tbsp vegetable oil
1 garlic clove, chopped
    finely
6 scallions, sliced
1 tsp chili paste
2 tbsp soy sauce
2 tbsp rice wine
4 tbsp smooth peanut
    butter
3 tbsp coconut milk

 extremely easy

serves 4

20 minutes

8–10 minutes

❶ Cut the carrots diagonally into thin slices. Cut the cauliflower into small florets, then slice the stem thinly. Slice the bok choy thickly. Cut the beans into 1¼ inch/ 3 cm lengths.

❷ Heat the oil in a large skillet or wok, and stir-fry the garlic and scallions for about 1 minute. Stir in the chili paste and cook for a few seconds.

❸ Add the carrots and cauliflower and stir-fry them for 2–3 minutes.

❹ Add the bok choy and beans, and stir-fry for another 2 minutes. Stir in the soy sauce and rice wine.

❺ Mix the peanut butter with the coconut milk and stir into the pan, then cook, stirring, for another minute. Serve immediately while still hot.

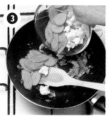

COOK'S TIP
It is important to cut the vegetables thinly into even-sized pieces so that they cook quickly and evenly. Prepare all the vegetables before you start to cook.

Chinese Vegetables with Yellow Bean Sauce

INGREDIENTS

1 eggplant
salt
2 tbsp vegetable oil
3 garlic cloves, crushed
4 scallions, chopped
1 small red bell pepper, deseeded and sliced thinly
4 baby corn, halved lengthwise
1 cup snow peas
7 oz/200 g Chinese mustard greens, shredded coarsely
15 oz/425 g canned Chinese straw mushrooms, drained
1 cup beansprouts
2 tbsp rice wine
2 tbsp yellow bean sauce
2 tbsp dark soy sauce
1 tsp chili sauce
1 tsp sugar
½ cup vegetable bouillon
1 tsp cornstarch
2 tsp water

❶ Trim the eggplant and cut into 2 inch/5 cm long, thin sticks. Place in a colander and sprinkle with salt, then let drain for 30 minutes. Rinse in cold water and dry with paper towels.

❷ Heat the oil in a skillet or a wok and stir-fry the garlic, scallions, and bell pepper over a high heat for 1 minute. Stir in the eggplant pieces and stir-fry for another minute, or until softened.

❸ Stir in the corn and snow peas, and stir-fry for about 1 minute. Add the mustard greens, mushrooms, and beansprouts, and stir-fry for 30 seconds.

❹ Mix together the rice wine, yellow bean sauce, soy sauce, chili sauce, and sugar, and add to the pan with the bouillon. Bring to a boil, stirring.

❺ Blend the cornstarch with the water slowly, to form a smooth paste. Stir quickly into the skillet or wok and cook for another minute. Serve immediately.

very easy

serves 4

15 minutes

10 minutes

Spiced Cashew Nut Curry

1½ cups unsalted cashew
    nuts
1 tsp coriander seeds
1 tsp cumin seeds
2 cardamom pods, crushed
1 tbsp sunflower oil
1 onion, sliced finely
1 garlic clove, crushed
1 small green chili,
    deseeded and chopped
1 cinnamon stick
½ tsp ground turmeric
4 tbsp coconut cream
1¼ cups hot vegetable
    bouillon
3 kaffir lime leaves,
    shredded finely
salt and pepper
boiled jasmine rice, to
    serve

 extremely easy

serves 4

10 minutes

35 minutes

❶ Soak the cashew nuts in cold water overnight. Drain thoroughly. Crush the coriander seeds, cumin seeds and cardamom pods with a pestle in a mortar.

❷ Heat the oil and stir-fry the onion and garlic for 2–3 minutes to soften, but not brown. Add the chili, crushed spices, cinnamon stick, and turmeric, and stir-fry for another minute.

❸ Add the coconut cream and the hot bouillon to the pan. Bring to a boil, then add the cashew nuts and lime leaves.

❹ Cover the pan, then lower the heat and simmer for about 20 minutes. Serve hot, accompanied by jasmine rice.

COOK'S TIP
Ground spices may be used in this recipe, but all spices give a better flavor when they are freshly crush with a mortar in a pestle.

Omelet Stuffed with Eggplants & Mushrooms

INGREDIENTS

3 tbsp vegetable oil
1 garlic clove, chopped
1 small onion, chopped
1 small eggplant, diced
½ small green bell
    pepper, deseeded and
    chopped
1 large dried Chinese
    black mushroom,
    soaked, drained and
    sliced
1 tomato, diced
1 tbsp light soy sauce
½ tsp sugar
¼ tsp ground black
    pepper
2 large eggs
salad greens, tomato
    wedges, and cucumber
    slices, to garnish

 very easy

serves 4

15 minutes

10 minutes

❶ Heat half the oil and cook the garlic over a high heat for 30 seconds. Add the onion and the eggplant and continue to stir-fry until golden.

❷ Add the green bell pepper and stir-fry for another minute to soften. Stir in the mushroom, tomato, soy sauce, sugar, and pepper. Remove from the skillet and keep hot.

❸ Beat the eggs together lightly. Heat the remaining oil, swirling to coat a wide area. Pour in the egg and swirl to set around the skillet.

❹ When the egg is set, spoon the filling into the center. Fold in the sides of the omelet to make a square parcel.

❺ Slide the omelet carefully onto a warmed dish and garnish with salad greens, tomato wedges, and cucumber slices. Serve hot.

COOK'S TIP
If you heat the skillet before adding the oil, and heat the oil before adding the ingredients, none of the ingredients will stick to the skillet.

Crispy Bean Curd with Chile & Soy Sauce

INGREDIENTS

10½ oz/300 g firm bean
    curd
2 tbsp vegetable oil
1 garlic clove, sliced
1 carrot, cut into short,
    thin sticks
½ green bell pepper,
    deseeded and cut into
    short, thin sticks
1 red bird's-eye chile,
    deseeded and
    chopped finely
2 tbsp soy sauce
1 tbsp lime juice
1 tbsp Thai fish sauce
1 tbsp soft light brown
    sugar
pickled garlic slices, to
    serve (optional)

extremely easy

serves 4

10 minutes

5–10 minutes

❶ Drain the bean curd and pat dry with paper towels. Cut into ¾ inch/2 cm cubes.

❷ Heat the oil in a wok and stir-fry the garlic for 1 minute. Remove the garlic and add the bean curd, then cook quickly until well browned, turning gently to brown on all sides.

❸ Lift out the bean curd, then drain well and keep hot. Stir the carrot and bell pepper into the wok and stir-fry for 1 minute.

❹ Spoon the carrot and bell peppers onto a dish and pile the bean curd on top.

❺ Mix together the chili, soy sauce, lime juice, fish sauce, and sugar, stirring until the sugar is dissolved.

❻ Spoon the sauce over the bean curd and serve topped, perhaps with slices of pickled garlic. Serve hot.

COOK'S TIP

Buy firm fresh bean curd for this dish—the silken type is softer, more like junket in texture and not firm enough to hold its shape well during cooking. It is better for adding to soups.

Refried Beans

INGREDIENTS

1 lb 2 oz/500 g dried
pinto or borlotti beans
sprig each of mint,
thyme, and parsley
1 onion, cut into chunks
½ cup vegetable oil or
4½ oz/125 g
shortening or dripping
1–2 onions, chopped
½ tsp ground cumin
salt
9 oz/250 g grated
Cheddar cheese
(optional)

❶ Soak the beans overnight. Drain, then place in a pan and cover with water and the herbs. Bring to a boil, then reduce the heat and simmer, covered, for 2 hours, or until the beans are tender. Add the onion and cook until the onion and beans are very tender. Put two-thirds of the cooked beans, with their cooking liquid, in a food processor and process to a purée. Stir in the remaining whole beans. Set aside.

❷ Heat the oil or fat in a skillet. Add the onions and cook until very soft. Sprinkle with cumin and salt to taste.

❸ Ladle in a cupful of the bean mixture, and cook, stirring, until the beans reduce to a thick mixture; the beans will darken as they cook. Continue adding the mixture, a ladleful at a time, stirring, and reducing the liquid before adding the next ladleful. You should end up with a thick, chunky purée.

❹ If using cheese, sprinkle it over the beans and cover until the heat in the skillet melts the cheese. Alternatively, place under a preheated broiler to melt the cheese. Serve at once.

extremely easy

serves 4

5–10 minute, plus 8 hours to soak

3 hours

Black Bean Nachos

1¼ cups dried black
   beans, or canned
   black beans, drained
6–8 oz/175–225 g grated
   cheese, such as
   Cheddar, Fonpana,
   romano, asiago, or a
   combination
about ¼ tsp cumin seeds
   or ground cumin
about 4 tbsp sour cream
pickled jalapeños, sliced
   thinly (optional)
1 tbsp chopped fresh
   cilantro
handful of shredded
   lettuce
tortilla chips, to serve

❶ If using dried black beans, soak the beans overnight, then drain. Put in a pan, then cover with water and bring to a boil. Boil for 10 minutes, then reduce the heat and simmer for about 1½ hours, or until tender. Drain well.

❷ Spread the beans over the bottom of a shallow ovenproof dish, then scatter the cheese over the top. Sprinkle with cumin, to taste.

❸ Bake in a preheated oven at 375°F/190°C for 10–15 minutes, or until the beans are cooked through and the cheese is bubbling and melted.

❹ Remove the beans and cheese from the oven, and spoon the sour cream on top. Add the jalapeños, if using, and sprinkle with fresh cilantro and lettuce.

❺ Arrange the tortilla chips around the beans, sticking them into the mixture. Serve the nachos at once.

extremely easy

serves 4

5–10 minutes,
plus 8 hours to
soak

2 hours

Potatoes with Goat Cheese & Chipotle Cream

INGREDIENTS

*2 lb 12 oz/1.25 kg baking
potatoes, peeled and
cut into chunks*
pinch of salt
pinch of sugar
¾ cups crème fraîche
*½ cup vegetable
bouillon*
*3 garlic cloves, chopped
finely*
*a few shakes of bottled
chipotle salsa, or
½ dried chipotle,
reconstituted,
deseeded, and sliced
thinly*
*8 oz/225 g goat cheese,
sliced*
*6 oz/175 g mozzarella or
Cheddar cheese,
grated*
*1¾ oz/50 g Parmesan or
romano cheese,
grated*
salt

❶ Put the potatoes in a pan of water with the salt and sugar. Bring to a boil and cook for about 10 minutes, or until they are half cooked.

❷ Combine the crème fraîche with the bouillon, garlic, and the chipotle salsa.

❸ Arrange half the potatoes in a casserole. Pour half the crème fraîche sauce over the potatoes and cover with the goat cheese. Top with the remaining potatoes and the sauce.

❹ Sprinkle with the grated mozzarella or Cheddar cheese, then with the grated Parmesan or the romano cheese.

❺ Bake in a preheated oven at 350°F/180°C, or until the potatoes are tender and the cheese topping is lightly golden and crisped in places. Serve at once.

extremely easy

serves 4

15 minutes

20 minutes

Vegetable Tostadas

vegetable oil, for frying
4 corn tortillas
2–3 tbsp extra-virgin
    olive oil or vegetable
    oil
2 potatoes, diced
1 carrot, diced
3 garlic cloves, chopped
    finely
1 red bell pepper,
    deseeded and diced
1 tsp mild chili powder
1 tsp paprika
½ tsp ground cumin
3–4 ripe tomatoes, diced
4 oz/115 g green beans,
    blanched and cut into
    bite-sized lengths
several large pinches
    dried oregano
14 oz/400 g cooked black
    beans, drained
8 oz/225 g crumbled feta
    cheese
3–4 leaves romaine
    lettuce, shredded
3–4 scallions, sliced
    thinly

❶ To make tostadas, cook the tortillas in a small amount of oil in a non-stick skillet until crisp.

❷ Heat the olive oil in a skillet, then add the potatoes and carrot, and cook until softened. Add the garlic, red bell pepper, chili powder, paprika, and cumin. Cook for 2–3 minutes, or until the peppers have softened.

❸ Add the tomatoes, green beans, and oregano. Cook for 8–10 minutes, or until the vegetables are tender and form a saucelike mixture. The mixture should not be too dry; add a little water if necessary, to keep it moist.

❹ Heat the black beans in a pan with a tiny amount of water, and keep warm. Reheat the tostadas under the broiler.

❺ Layer the beans over the hot tostadas, then sprinkle with the cheese and top with a few spoonfuls of the hot vegetables in sauce. Serve at once, each tostada sprinkled with the lettuce and scallions.

very easy

serves 4

15 minutes

20 minutes

Red Rice Pilaf with Roasted Vegetables

½ cup olive oil
grated zest and juice of
    1 orange
2 tbsp balsamic vinegar
2 tsp coriander seeds
1 bay leaf
½ tsp crushed dried
    chilis, or to taste
8–10 small raw beets,
    halved
9 oz/250 g shallots
6–8 baby parsnips
4–6 baby carrots
1 tsp chopped fresh
    rosemary leaves
14 oz/400 g red rice
3¾ cups hot bouillon
1 red onion
1 small carrot, cut into
    short, thin sticks
1 leek, cut into rounds
½ cup pine nuts, roasted
1 tsp light brown sugar
1 cup dried cranberries
    soaked in boiling
    water for 15 minutes
1–2 tbsp chopped cilantro
salt and pepper

TO SERVE
1 cup soured cream
2 tbsp chopped roasted
    walnuts

easy

serves 4

25 minutes

55 minutes

❶ Put about 4 tablespoons of the olive oil in a large bowl and whisk in the orange zest and juice, vinegar, and bay leaf. Crush the coriander seeds and chilis lightly, and whisk them in. Trim the beets, shallots, parsnips, and carrots, add them to the bowl, and stir to coat well.

❷ Turn into a roasting pan and roast in a preheated oven at 400°F/200°C for 45–55 minutes turning occasionally. Remove from the oven, then sprinkle with the rosemary and salt and pepper, and keep warm.

❸ Put the rice in a large pan with the hot bouillon. Place over a medium–high heat and bring to a boil; reduce the heat to low and simmer, covered, for about 40 minutes, or until the rice is tender and the bouillon absorbed. Remove from the heat, but do not uncover.

❹ Heat the remaining oil in a large pan. Add the onion and carrot strips, and cook for 8–10 minutes, or until tender. Add the leek, pine nuts, brown sugar, and cilantro, and cook for 2–3 minutes, or until the vegetables are lightly caramelized. Drain the cranberries and stir into the vegetable mixture with the rice. Season to taste.

❺ Arrange the vegetables and rice on a plate and top with the cream. Sprinkle with the chopped walnuts and serve.

Curried Rice Patties with Tahini Dressing

INGREDIENTS

½ tsp salt
⅓ cup basmati rice
2 tbsp olive oil
1 red onion, chopped
2 garlic cloves
2 tsp curry powder
½ tsp crushed dried chili
   flakes
1 small red bell pepper,
   deseeded, and diced
1 cup frozen peas
1 small leek, chopped
1 ripe tomato, skinned,
   and deseeded
310 g/11 oz canned
   garbanzo beans,
   drained and rinsed
1½ cups fresh white
   bread crumbs
2 tbsp chopped cilantro
1 egg, lightly beaten
vegetable oil, for cooking
salt and pepper

DRESSING
½ cup tahini
2 garlic cloves
½ tsp ground cumin
pinch of cayenne pepper
5 tbsp lemon juice
drizzle of extra-virgin
   olive oil
about ½ cup water

❶ To make the dressing, blend the tahini, garlic, cumin, cayenne, and lemon juice in a food processor until creamy. Slowly pour in the oil, then gradually add water to make a creamy dressing.

❷ Bring a pan of water to a boil. Add the salt and sprinkle in the rice; simmer for 15–20 minutes, or until the rice is just tender. Drain and rinse, then set aside.

❸ Heat the olive oil in a large pan. Add the onion and garlic, and cook until they begin to soften. Stir in the curry powder and chili, and cook for 2 minutes. Add the pepper, peas, leek, and chopped tomato flesh, and cook gently for 7 minutes, or until tender. Set aside.

❹ Process the garbanzo beans in the food processor until smooth. Add half the vegetables and process again. Transfer to a large bowl and add the remaining vegetable mixture, bread crumbs, chopped fresh cilantro, and egg; mix well. Stir in the rice and season well. Chill for 1 hour, then shape into 4–6 patties.

❺ Cook the patties in oil for 6–8 minutes, or until golden, and serve with the dressing, garnished with slices of cucumber and wedges of lime.

easy

serves 4

20 minutes

40 minutes,
plus 1 hour
to chill

❶

❸

Spicy Potato & Rice Pilaf

INGREDIENTS

1 cup basmati rice,
  soaked in cold water
  for 20 minutes
2 tbsp vegetable oil
½–¾ tsp cumin seeds
8 oz/225 g potatoes, cut
  into ½ inch/1 cm
  pieces
2 cups frozen peas,
  defrosted
1 green chile, deseeded
  and sliced thinly
  (optional)
½ tsp salt
1 tsp garam masala
½ tsp ground turmeric
¼ tsp cayenne pepper
2½ cups water
2 tbsp chopped fresh
  cilantro
1 red onion, chopped
  finely
plain yogurt, to serve

❶ Rinse the soaked rice under cold running water until the water runs clear, then drain and set aside.

❷ Heat the oil in a large heavy-based pan over a medium–high heat. Add the cumin seeds and stir for about 10 seconds, or until the seeds jump and color.

❸ Add the potatoes, peas, and chile (if using) and stir-fry for 3 minutes, or until the potatoes are just beginning to soften.

❹ Add the rice and cook, stirring often, until well coated and beginning to turn translucent. Stir in the salt, garam masala, turmeric, and cayenne pepper, then add the water. Bring to a boil, stirring once or twice, then reduce the heat to medium and simmer, covered, until most of the water is absorbed and the surface is filled with little steam-holes. Do not stir the mixture.

❺ Reduce the heat to very low and, if possible, raise the pan about 1 inch/2.5 cm above the heat source by resting it on a ring. Cover, and steam for about 10 minutes longer. Remove from the heat, then uncover, put a clean dish towel or paper towels over the rice, and re-cover. Stand for 5 minutes.

❻ Put the mixture in a bowl and sprinkle with the cilantro and onion. Serve hot with yogurt handed round separately.

very easy

serves 4

10 minutes,
plus 20 minutes
to soak

35 minutes

Arugula & Tomato Risotto with Mozzarella

2 tbsp olive oil
2 tbsp unsalted butter
1 large onion, chopped finely
2 garlic cloves, chopped finely
1¾ cups arborio rice
½ cup dry white vermouth (optional)
6¼ cups vegetable bouillon, simmering
6 vine-ripened or Italian plum tomatoes, deseeded and chopped
4½ oz/125 g arugula
handful of fresh basil leaves
1⅓ cups freshly grated Parmesan cheese
8 oz/225 g fresh Italian buffalo mozzarella, grated coarsely or diced
salt and pepper

❶ Heat the oil and half the butter in a large skillet. Add the onion and cook for about 2 minutes, or until it just begins to soften. Stir in the garlic and rice, and cook, stirring frequently, until the rice is translucent and well coated.

❷ Pour in the white vermouth, if using; it will bubble and steam rapidly and evaporate almost immediately. Add a ladleful (about 1 cup) of the simmering bouillon, and cook, stirring constantly, until it is absorbed.

❸ Continue adding the bouillon, about half a ladleful at a time, letting each addition be absorbed before adding the next. Never let the rice cook dry.

❹ Just before the rice is tender, stir in the chopped tomatoes and the arugula. Shred the basil leaves and stir into the risotto immediately. Continue to cook, adding more bouillon, until the risotto is creamy and the rice is tender but firm to the bite.

❺ Remove from the heat and stir in the remaining butter, the Parmesan cheese, and the mozzarella. Season to taste with salt and pepper. Cover and stand for about 1 minute. Serve the risotto immediately, before the mozzarella has melted completely.

very easy

serves 4

15 minutes

35 minutes

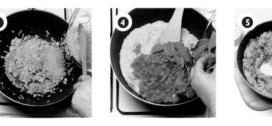

Cheese-Topped Risotto Tart with Spinach

INGREDIENTS

1⅓ cups all-purpose flour
½ tsp salt
1 tsp superfine sugar
½ cup unsalted butter,
* diced*
1 egg yolk, beaten with
* 2 tbsp iced water*

FILLING

1 quantity basic cooked
* risotto, still warm*
* (follow recipe on*
* page 62, omitting*
* tomatoes, rocket,*
* basil, and mozzarella)*
9 oz/250 g spinach,
* cooked, drained very*
* well and chopped*
2 tbsp heavy cream
8 oz/225 g mozzarella,
* preferably buffalo*
* mozzarella*
¾ cup freshly grated
* Parmesan cheese*

❶ To make the pastry, sift the flour, salt, and sugar into a large bowl and sprinkle the butter on top. Rub the butter into the flour until the mixture forms coarse crumbs. Sprinkle in the egg mixture and stir to make a dough.

❷ Gather the dough into a ball, then wrap in plastic wrap and chill for at least 1 hour.

❸ Roll out the pastry gently to a thickness of about ⅛ inch/ 3 mm, then use it to line a lightly greased 9–10 inch/ 23–25 cm tart pan with a removable base. Prick the bottom with a fork and chill for 1 hour.

❹ Cover the tart case with baking paper and fill with baking beans. Bake blind in a preheated oven at 400°F/200°C for about 20 minutes, or until the pastry is set and the edge is golden. Remove the beans and paper, and set aside. Reduce the oven temperature to 350°F/180°C.

❺ Put the risotto in a bowl and stir in the spinach, cream, half the mozzarella, and half the Parmesan cheese. Spoon the mixture into the tart case and smooth it over. Sprinkle the remaining cheeses on top.

❻ Bake for 12–15 minutes, or until cooked through and golden. Cool slightly on a wire rack, then serve warm.

easy

serves 4

20 minutes,
plus 1 hour
to chill

35 minutes

Salads & Side Dishes

A recipe that will change the image of lentils, often accused of being boring and a staple food of cranks, is Lentils Simmered with Fruit. Apples, pineapples, tomatoes, and even bananas go into this intriguing dish, which is spiced with cayenne pepper. And if you have never liked broad beans, you may be surprised by Fava Beans with Feta & Lemon—tossed in a delicious olive oil and lemon dressing with fresh dill.

Thai-Style Carrot & Mango Salad

4 carrots
1 small, ripe mango
7 oz/200 g firm bean
   curd
1 tbsp fresh chives,
   chopped

DRESSING
2 tbsp orange juice
1 tbsp lime juice
1 tsp clear honey
½ tsp orange-flower
   water
1 tsp sesame oil
1 tsp sesame seeds,
   toasted

❶ Peel the carrots and grate them roughly. Peel and pit the mango and slice it thinly.

❷ Cut the bean curd into ½ inch/1 cm dice-shaped pieces and toss them with the carrots and mango in a wide salad bowl.

❸ For the dressing, place all the ingredients in a screw-top jar and shake well to mix evenly.

❹ Pour the dressing over the salad and toss well to coat the salad evenly.

❺ Just before serving, toss the salad lightly and sprinkle with chives. Serve immediately.

extremely easy

serves 4

10 minutes

0 minutes

Rice with Black Beans

INGREDIENTS

1 onion, chopped
5 garlic cloves, chopped
1 cup vegetable bouillon
2 tbsp vegetable oil
scant 1 cup long-grain
   rice
½ tsp ground cumin
1 cup liquid from cooking
   black beans salt and
   pepper

TO GARNISH
3–5 scallions, sliced
   thinly
2 tbsp chopped fresh
   cilantro leaves

❶ Put the onion in a blender with the garlic and bouillon and blend the ingredients until they have the consistency of a thick sauce.

❷ Heat the oil in a heavy-based pan and cook the rice until it is golden. Add the onion mixture, with the cooking liquid from the black beans (including any beans floating in it). Add the cumin, with salt and pepper to taste.

❸ Cover the pan and cook over a medium-low heat for about 10 minutes, or until the rice is just tender and is evenly coloured by the black bean liquid.

❹ Fluff up the rice with a fork, and let rest for 5 minutes, covered. Serve sprinkled with the scallions and cilantro.

extremely easy

serves 4

10 minutes

15 minutes,
plus 5 minutes
to stand

Lentils Simmered with Fruit

INGREDIENTS

generous ½ cup brown or
green lentils
about 4 cups water
2 tbsp vegetable oil
3 small to medium-sized
onions, chopped
4 garlic cloves, chopped
coarsely
1 large tart apple,
chopped coarsely
about ¼ ripe pineapple,
skin removed and
chopped coarsely
2 tomatoes, deseeded
and diced
1 almost ripe banana, cut
into bite-sized pieces
salt
cayenne pepper, to taste
fresh parsley sprig, to
garnish

❶ Combine the lentils with the water in a pan, then bring to a boil. Reduce the heat and simmer over a low heat for about 40 minutes, or until the lentils are tender. Do not let them overcook so they become mushy.

❷ Meanwhile, heat the oil in a skillet and cook the onions and garlic until they are lightly browned and softened. Add the apple and continue to cook until golden. Add the pineapple and heat it through, stirring continuously, then add the tomatoes. Cook over a medium heat until the mixture has thickened, stirring occasionally.

❸ Drain the lentils, reserving 1 cup of the cooking liquid. Add the drained lentils to the sauce, stirring in the reserved liquid if necessary. Heat through for a minute to mingle the flavors.

❹ Add the banana to the pan, then season with salt and cayenne pepper. Serve garnished with parsley.

very easy

serves 4

25 minutes

1 hour
20 minutes

Gazpacho Rice Salad

INGREDIENTS

extra-virgin olive oil
1 onion, chopped finely
4 garlic cloves, chopped
    finely
1 cup long-grain white
    rice or basmati
1½ cups vegetable
    bouillon or water
1½ tsp dried thyme
3 tbsp sherry vinegar
1 tsp Dijon mustard
1 tsp honey or sugar
1 red bell pepper, cored
    and chopped
½ yellow bell pepper,
    cored and chopped
½ green bell pepper,
    cored and chopped
1 red onion, chopped
    finely
3 tomatoes, deseeded
    and chopped
2–3 tbsp chopped
    flatleaf parsley
salt and pepper

TO SERVE
12 cherry tomatoes,
    halved
12 black olives, pitted
    and chopped coarsely
1 tbsp slivered almonds,
    toasted

very easy

serves 4

25 minutes

55 minutes,
plus 30 minutes
to stand

❶ Heat 2 tablespoons of the oil in a large pan. Add the onion and cook for 2 minutes, stirring frequently, until the onion begins to soften. Stir in half the garlic and cook for another minute.

❷ Add the rice, stirring well to coat, and cook for about 2 minutes, or until translucent. Stir in the bouillon and half the thyme, and bring to a boil. Season with salt and pepper. Simmer very gently, covered, for about 20 minutes, or until tender. Stand, still covered, for about 15 minutes, then uncover and cool completely.

❸ Whisk the vinegar with the remaining garlic and thyme, mustard, honey, and salt and pepper in a large bowl. Slowly whisk in about ⅓ cup of the olive oil. Using a fork, fluff the rice into the vinaigrette.

❹ Add the bell peppers, red onion, chopped tomatoes, and parsley, then toss and season.

❺ Transfer to a serving bowl and garnish with the cherry tomatoes, olives, and almonds. Serve warm.

Coconut-Scented Brown Rice

❶ Bring the water to a boil in a heavy-based pan and whisk in the coconut milk. Return the liquid to a boil, then add the salt and sprinkle in the rice.

❷ Pare 2–3 strips of lemon zest and add to the pan with the cinnamon stick and the cloves.

❸ Reduce the heat to low, then cover and simmer gently for about 45 minutes, or until the rice is tender and the liquid is completely absorbed. Uncover and stand the rice over high heat for about 1 minute, to let any steam escape and the rice dry out a little.

❹ Remove the cloves, if preferred, sprinkle with the herbs and coconut, if using, then fork into a warmed serving bowl and serve.

extremely easy

serves 4

5 minutes

1 hour

COOK'S TIP
This technique can be used to cook white rice as well, but the fuller flavor of brown rice works well with the warm flavor of the spices.

Fava Beans with Feta & Lemon

INGREDIENTS

1 lb 2 oz/500 g shelled
  fava beans
4 tbsp extra-virgin olive
  oil
1 tbsp lemon juice
1 tbsp finely chopped
  fresh dill, plus a little
  extra for garnishing
2¼ oz/60 g feta cheese,
  drained and diced
salt and pepper
lemon wedges, to serve

very easy

serves 4

10–15 minutes

10 minutes

❶ Bring a pan of water to a boil. Add the fava beans and cook them for about 2 minutes, or until they are tender. Drain the cooked beans well.

❷ When the beans are cool enough to handle, remove and discard the outer skins, to reveal the bright green beans underneath (see Cook's Tip). Put the shelled beans in a serving bowl.

❸ Stir together the olive oil and lemon juice, then season with salt and pepper to taste. Pour the warm beans over the mixture, add the dill, then stir. Adjust the seasoning, if necessary.

❹ If serving hot, toss with the feta cheese and sprinkle with extra dill. Alternatively, let cool and chill until required. Remove from the refrigerator 10 minutes before serving, season to taste, and sprinkle with the feta and extra dill. Serve with lemon wedges.

COOK'S TIP

If you are lucky enough to have very young fava beans at the start of the season, you do not need to remove the outer skin.

Green Tabbouleh

INGREDIENTS

1¼ cups bulgar wheat
7 oz/200 g cucumber
6 scallions
½ oz/15 g fresh flatleaf
    parsley
1 unwaxed lemon
about 2 tbsp garlic-
    flavored olive oil
salt and pepper

❶ Bring a kettle of water to a boil. Place the bulgar wheat in a heatproof bowl, then pour over 2½ cups boiling water and cover. Set aside for at least 20 minutes, or until the wheat absorbs the water and becomes tender.

❷ Meanwhile, cut the cucumber in half lengthwise, then cut each half into 3 strips lengthwise. Using a teaspoon, scoop out and discard the seeds. Chop the cucumber strips into bite-sized pieces and put in a serving bowl.

❸ Trim the top of the green parts of each of the scallions, then cut each in half lengthwise. Chop finely and add to the cucumber.

❹ Place the parsley on a cutting board and sprinkle with salt. Chop the leaves and stalks very finely and add to the bowl with the cucumber and onions. Grate the lemon zest into the bowl.

❺ When the bulgar wheat is cool enough to handle, squeeze out excess water, either with your hands or by pressing it through a strainer, then add it to the other ingredients.

❻ Cut the lemon in half and squeeze the juice of one half over the salad. Add 2 tablespoons of the garlic-flavored oil, and stir all the ingredients together. Season with salt and pepper to taste and add extra lemon juice or oil if needed. Cover, and chill until the salad is required.

very easy

serves 4

20 minutes,
plus 20 minutes
to soak

0 minutes

Zucchinis & Tomatoes with Green Chile Vinaigrette

INGREDIENTS

1 large mild green chile,
or a combination of
1 green bell pepper
and ½–1 green chile
4 zucchini, sliced
2–3 garlic cloves,
chopped finely
pinch sugar
¼ tsp ground cumin
2 tbsp white wine
vinegar
4 tbsp extra-virgin olive
oil
2–3 tbsp cilantro
4 ripe tomatoes, diced
or sliced
salt and pepper

❶ Roast the mild chile, or the combination of the green bell pepper and chile, in a heavy-based ungreased skillet or under a preheated broiler until the skin is charred. Place in a plastic bag, twist to seal well, and let the mixture stand for 20 minutes.

❷ Peel the skin from the chile and pepper, if using, then remove the seeds and slice the flesh. Set aside.

❸ Bring about 2 inches/5 cm water to a boil in the bottom of a steamer. Add the zucchini to the top part of the steamer, then cover and steam for about 5 minutes, or until just tender.

❹ Meanwhile, combine the garlic, sugar, cumin, vinegar, olive oil, and cilantro in a bowl. Stir the chile and pepper (if using) into the mixture, then season the dressing with salt and pepper to taste.

❺ Arrange the zucchini and tomatoes in a serving bowl or on a plate and spoon the chile dressing over them. Toss the vegetables gently together, and serve.

very easy

serves 4

15 minutes,
plus 20 minutes
to stand

10 minutes

82

Desserts

Vegetarians love puddings as much as everyone else. However, they may be more inclined to use quality unrefined and organic ingredients, which are now widely available and give the best results. The best chocolate, which has a high proportion of cocoa solids, will produce a better Saucy Chocolate Pudding than cheap cooking chocolate, while a pale golden superfine sugar will add a special flavor and character to the Lemon & Lime Syllabub. The recipes in the following pages use milk and cream, nuts and berries to create imaginative desserts.

Almond Rice Custard

INGREDIENTS

¾ cup whole blanched
   almonds
4 cups milk
scant ¼ cup rice flour
pinch of salt
¼ cup sugar
½ tsp almond extract or
   1 tbsp almond-flavor
   liqueur
toasted slivered
   almonds, to decorate

TO SERVE (OPTIONAL)
12 oz/350 g fresh
   strawberries, sliced,
   sprinkled with 2 tbsp
   sugar and chilled

❶ Put the almonds in a food processor and process until a thick paste forms. Bring 1 cup of the milk to a boil. Gradually pour into the almond paste, with the machine running, until the mixture is smooth. Let stand for about 10 minutes.

❷ Combine the rice flour, salt, and sugar in a large bowl, then stir in about 4–5 tablespoons of the milk to form a smooth paste.

❸ Bring the remaining milk to a boil in a pan. Pour the hot milk into the rice flour paste and stir constantly, then return the mixture to the pan and bring to a boil. Reduce the heat and simmer for about 10 minutes, or until smooth and thickened. Remove from the heat.

❹ Strain the almond milk through a very fine strainer into the simmering rice custard, pressing through the almonds with the back of a spoon. Return to the heat and simmer for 7–10 minutes, or until it becomes thick.

❺ Remove from the heat and stir in the almond extract. Cool slightly, stirring, then pour into individual bowls. Sprinkle with the almonds and serve with the strawberries, if wished. Chill to serve later, if preferred—the custard will thicken as it cools.

very easy

serves 4

15 minutes,
plus 10 minutes
to stand

30 minutes

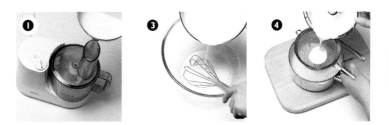

Saucy Chocolate Pudding

INGREDIENTS

1¼ cups milk
2¾ oz/75 g semisweet
   chocolate
½ tsp vanilla extract
7 tbsp superfine sugar
generous ⅓ cup butter
1¼ cups self-rising flour
2 tbsp cocoa powder
confectioners' sugar,
   to dust

SAUCE
3 tbsp cocoa powder
4 tbsp light muscovado
   sugar
1¼ cups boiling water

❶ Grease a 1½ pint/850 ml ovenproof dish lightly.

❷ Place the milk in a small pan. Break the chocolate into pieces and add to the milk. Heat the mixture gently, stirring until the chocolate melts. Let cool slightly and stir in the vanilla extract.

❸ Beat together the superfine sugar and butter in a bowl until light and fluffy. Strain the flour and cocoa powder together. Add to the bowl with the chocolate milk and beat until smooth, using an electric whisk if you have one. Pour the mixture into the prepared dish.

❹ To make the sauce, mix together the cocoa powder and sugar. Add a little boiling water and mix to a smooth paste, then stir in the remaining water. Pour the sauce over the pudding, but do not mix in.

❺ Place the dish onto a cookie sheet and bake in a preheated oven, 350°F/180°C, for 40 minutes, or until dry on top and springy to the touch. Let stand for about 5 minutes, then dust with a little confectioners' sugar just before serving.

very easy

serves 4

15 minutes

50 minutes, plus
5 minutes
to stand

Chocolate Hazelnut Pots

INGREDIENTS

2 eggs
2 egg yolks
1 tbsp superfine sugar
1 tsp cornstarch
2½ cups milk
3 oz/85 g dark chocolate
4 tbsp chocolate and
   hazelnut spread

TO DECORATE
grated chocolate or large
   chocolate curls

very easy

serves 4

15 minutes

55 minutes

❶ Beat together the eggs, egg yolks, superfine sugar, and cornstarch until well combined. Heat the milk until it is almost boiling.

❷ Pour the milk gradually onto the eggs, whisking as you do so. Melt the chocolate with the chocolate and hazelnut spread in a bowl set over a pan of gently simmering water. When the chocolate has melted completely into the spread, whisk the mixture into the eggs.

❸ Pour into 6 small ovenproof dishes and cover the dishes with foil. Place them in a roasting pan. Fill the pan with boiling water to come halfway up the sides of the dishes.

❹ Bake the dishes in a preheated oven, 325°F/160°C, for 35–40 minutes, or until the custard is just set. Remove from the pan and cool, then chill until required. Serve decorated with grated chocolate or chocolate curls.

COOK'S TIP
This dish is traditionally made in little *pots de crème*, individual ovenproof dishes with a lid. You can use custard pots or make the dessert in one large dish and cook it for about 1 hour to set it.

Berry Cheesecake

BASE
6 tbsp vegetarian
    margarine
6 oz/175 g oatmeal
    biscuits
¾ cup shredded coconut

TOPPING
1½ tsp gelatin
9 tbsp cold water
½ cup evaporated milk
1 egg
6 tbsp light brown sugar
2 cups soft cream cheese
1¾ cups mixed berries
2 tbsp clear honey

 very easy

 serves 4

25 minutes, plus
2 hours to chill

10 minutes

❶ Put the margarine in a pan and heat until melted. Put the biscuits in a food processor and blend until smooth, or crush finely with a rolling pin. Stir into the margarine with the coconut.

❷ Press the mixture into a base-lined 8 inch/20 cm spring-form pan and chill while preparing the filling.

❸ To make the topping, sprinkle the gelatin over the water and stir to dissolve. Bring to a boil and boil for 2 minutes. Let cool slightly.

❹ Put the milk, egg, sugar, and soft cream cheese in a bowl and beat until smooth. Stir in ¼ cup of the berries. Stir in the gelatin in a stream, stirring constantly, until fully incorporated.

❺ Spoon the mixture onto the biscuit base and return to the refrigerator for 2 hours, or until set.

❻ Remove the cheesecake from the pan and transfer to a serving plate. Arrange the remaining berries on top of the cheesecake and drizzle the honey over the top. Serve.

COOK'S TIP
Warm the honey slightly to make it runnier and easier to drizzle.

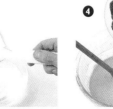

Lemon & Lime Syllabub

¼ cup superfine sugar
grated zest and juice of
1 small lemon
grated zest and juice of
1 small lime
4 tbsp Marsala wine or
medium sherry
1¼ cups heavy cream
lime and lemon zest, to
decorate

❶ Put the sugar, fruit juices and zest, and the wine or sherry in a bowl, mix well, then let infuse for 2 hours.

❷ Add the cream to the mixture and whisk until it just holds its shape.

❸ Spoon the mixture into 4 tall serving glasses and chill in the refrigerator for 2 hours.

❹ Decorate with lime and lemon zest, and serve.

extremely easy

serves 4

10 hours,
plus 2 hours
to infuse

0 minutes

COOK'S TIP
Replace the heavy
cream with plain yogurt
for a healthier version
of this dessert, or use
half quantities of both.
Whisk the cream before
adding it to the yogurt.

94